IMAGES
of England

STECHFORD, WARD END
AND WASHWOOD HEATH

Bromford Lane.

IMAGES
of England

STECHFORD, WARD END AND WASHWOOD HEATH

Marian Baxter

TEMPUS

Washwood Heath Road and Bromford Lane at the Fox and Goose public house, September 1933.

First published 2002

Tempus Publishing Limited
The Mill, Brimscombe Port,
Stroud, Gloucestershire, GL5 2QG

British Library Cataloguing in Publication Data.
A catalogue record for this book is available from the British Library.

ISBN 0 7524 2674 5

Typesetting and origination by Tempus Publishing Limited
Printed in Great Britain by Midway Colour Print, Wiltshire

Contents

Criterion Plates Papers Firm Limited (formerly The Birmingham Photographic Company), Albert Road in around 1955. Built in 1896, the building was demolished in 1971.

Acknowledgements

My thanks in preparing this volume goes to the Local Studies and History Department of Birmingham Reference Library, for use of their collection of photographs.

A special thanks to Paul who, when I was getting desperate to find enough photographs, divulged the whereabouts of boxes of un-indexed photographs of all the areas I needed hitherto unknown to me. Thanks Paul.

I feel I should acknowledge the main sources used in putting together the volume: Birmingham Museum and Art Gallery, *Yardley Through the Camera, 1890–1900*. Carl Chin, *One Thousand Years of Brum*, F.P. Corden, *Stechford, Glebe Farm, Lea Hall and Tile Cross*. Jose Jukes, *Memories of Old Ward End*. Without the background information from these books I would have found it very difficult to put this book together. Thanks also to Geoff Cashmore for his patience and his help in the proof reading.

While every attempt has been made to ensure the information in this book is correct, I have used other people's works, newspaper cuttings and miscellaneous articles, as well as my own views. It has not always been possible to verify every piece of information used.

Introduction

When Tempus suggested a photographic book for their archive series on the areas of Stechford, Ward End and Washwood Heath I immediately volunteered. As I was born in the first house in Old Farm Road, Stechford, and lived there until I was sixteen, I felt that searching out old photographs would reawaken many of my forgotten memories of the area.

It proved to be a difficult task. I found that in trying to cover Glebe Farm, Hodge Hill, Stechford, Ward End and Washwood Heath it was almost impossible to define boundaries. In his book *Last Tram Down the Village*, Ray Tennant sums up the difficulties. He writes, 'Washwood Heath Road was the main thoroughfare which traversed it [Ward End] and for this reason many people referred to the area as Washwood Heath, and so all through my childhood years I never knew whether I lived in Ward End or Washwood Heath.' I always thought I lived in Glebe Farm but I was never sure where Stechford started, and the postal address was always Stechford. The areas covered in this book do not conform to the municipal wards so while I have grouped the photographs into areas, I have not followed any boundaries except my own.

The official boundaries for the areas are quite distinctive. The 1991 census shows that 25,167 people make up the ward of Hodge Hill. It lies east of the city and three wards make up the Hodge Hill Constituency. The ward consists mainly of established residential areas and also includes a number of important areas of open space, the largest of which is the Cole valley. The Fox and Goose is the main shopping area. Hodge Hill itself contains few industrial areas, although the Bromford Estate lies just north of the ward. Washwood Heath, which includes Ward End, is one on the three wards that make up the Hodge Hill Constituency. The 1991 census shows a population of 28,219. The ward stretches from Saltley Gate to the A4040, the 'outer circle', and includes North Saltley, Ward End, Washwood Heath and Alum Rock. Although predominantly residential, the ward also includes substantial industrial areas, which now form part of the Heartland's. The ward supports a wide range of social, community and religious facilities. Within the ward were some of the cities best-known companies and the largest employers including Metro-Cammell.

Stechford is part of Yardley, which has a population of 23,181 in the 1991 census. Yardley is predominantly a residential area, which includes the communities of Lea Hall, Stechford and Garretts Green. Although Yardley as a whole has no large industrial site, the closure of the Parkinson Cowan works dealt a blow to the economy of the Stechford area.

The growth of the areas covered in this book is very similar to those of the other surrounding areas. From the nineteenth-century village nucleus, they grew into tight early twentieth-century urban communities. However it is still difficult to imagine Stechford and Ward End today as villages surrounded by fields and country lanes. It is equally hard to think of Washwood Heath being chosen for the execution of eight men in 1802 because of its desolate state.

Some of these early images have, luckily, been recorded and the photographs in the first chapter of this book are drawn from an extensive collection taken by a Yardley man, Mr George Wilkes. Originally presented to the Birmingham Museum and Art Gallery by Mr F.H. Viney in 1957 they were passed to the Local Studies Department in Birmingham Central Library. Most of the information used in this chapter is taken from the booklet *Yardley Through the Camera, 1800-1900*, published by the Birmingham Museum and Art Gallery in 1957.

The photographs are remarkable not only for their technical quality but also for their incredible record showing farming methods and the equipment used in and around Stechford in the nineteenth century. They illustrate the farming year from ploughing and sowing the seed to the harvest of the hay and the corn. Other photographs used from this collection throughout this book show the conditions of the roads and country lanes at that time, people at leisure and in celebration. Some of the photographs show many old buildings and farms long since gone. The quiet village street, the fields and woodlands at the turn of the nineteenth century of all the areas covered in this book stand in complete contrast to the busy suburbs of the present day.

One

Farming in and around Stechford, 1890–1900

Wash Lane, between Stechford and Hay Mills.

Reaping the corn. Near the site of the present Francis Road and Morden Road. The machine seen in both photographs is an early reaper-binder.

The reaping machines could not reach the edges of the fields by the hedges, so the scythe was still employed to cut the corn near to the edge.

After cutting the corn, the sheaves were built into stooks, which were left to dry in the sun for several days.

The corn standing in rows of stooks.

Loading the wagon with the dry stooks.

The corn was built into ricks which where built on raised platforms to protect it from the damp and the vermin, and to allow air circulation. The ricks were thatched to protect the corn from the elements.

Field House Farm. This photograph shows an early threshing machine driven by the traction engine behind.

Harnessing the plough at Morris's Farm. The balance plough carried two sets of cutting equipment and was normally used on hilly ground.

Field House Farm. An iron-framed plough being drawn by three horses in tandem.

Above and below: The Yardley area was noted for its heavy soil and because of this, teams of three or four horses were used to pull the iron-framed plough.

Above and below: A horse-drawn seed drill sowing the seed.

An early horse-drawn mowing machine mowing the hay.

Near the River Cole, Stechford. Once the hay had been cut it was tossed for several days with a hay tedder, this enabled the cut grass to dry. Each night it was racked into windrows and cocked.

Near to the River Cole, Stechford. When dry, the hay was loaded onto the hay waggons with pitchforks.

Once the hay had been racked into windrows it was ready for loading onto the hay waggon.

The hay was gathered into rows with large drag-rakes (above) before loading onto the hay waggon with the pitchforks (below).

Thatching the haystack. This was done to protect the hay from the weather.

Two

Stechford

Stechford village and schools, c. 1905.

The Village, Stechford. Early spellings show Stechford as Stirchford and Stychford; the name was probably derived from Stachia, an old term for a dam made up of stakes and/or to stop a watercourse.

Market Place, Stechford. Stechford's history is very much included in with that of Yardley. Sometime around 1300, William of Berwode granted lands in Wodidbromwis to Alice, daughter of Adam Smith. Twenty-six years before, Stychforde was described as a hamlet, whilst in 1345 it was spelt as Stycheforde.

Horse and wagon, Lower Stechford. According to Carl Chinn, the district remained named Stirchford until the mid-nineteenth century, when the local railway station was wrongly spelt as Stechford.

Lower Stechford. The cottage in the centre of the photograph shows a timber-framed gable indicating a much earlier building.

Old Stechford. Lancers travelling along the dusty road.

Stechford Farm, 1925.

Wash End Farm, Stechford. In the 1920s, Stechford was remembered as 'Very much a village surrounded by fields, many farms, country lanes and ponds.'

Stechford Hall. Stechford Hall was actually in Castle Bromwich near to where Beaufort Avenue is today.

War Memorial, Five Ways, Stechford. 'Erected by public subscription to the immortal memory of the men of Stechford who fell in the Great War. 1914-1918.'

View across the Cole Valley, near Albert Road. Compare this photograph with the one below. It is the same view taken only a few years later.

A wedding in Morden Road. The chimney of the Yardley Road Fever Hospital can be seen in the distance.

Albert Road (undated).

Albert Road in 1957.

Albert Road. The urbanization of Stechford started in the last quarter of the nineteenth century. By the 1890s, Stechford village lay between Stechford station and Victoria Road, although Albert Road and Lyttleton Road were in existence.

Albert Road, May 1955.

Typical housing in Albert Road, March 1957.

B.R. Laundry in Albert Road, June 1961.

Telco Pressings, Albert Road, June 1975.

Albert Road at the junction of Station Road in June 1975.

All Saints Church, Albert Road. All Saints Church was opened as an iron mission church of Saint Edburgh's, Yardley, in 1887, costing £737. It became known as All Saints Church in 1892. The new church was built of brick, with terracotta facings in the Decorated style and consisted of a chancel, nave, lady-chapel, aisles and vestries. It was designed by J.A Chatwin. Lady Newport laid a memorial stone and the church was dedicated as All Saints in 1898 and consecrated in 1932. The church was completed in 1937 with the addition of an apsidal baptistery and west porch, presumably part of the original design. It closely resembles the contemporary Saint Mark's at Washwood Heath, by the same architect.

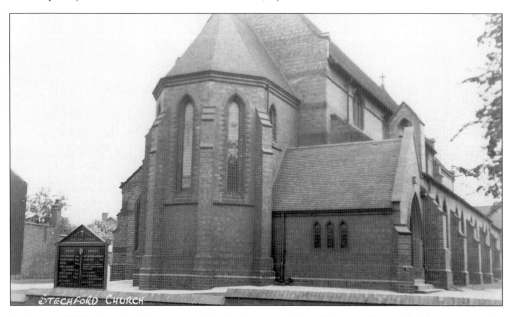

In August 1972 the church was struck by lightning and a gable was damaged.

The interior of All Saints Church.

Frederick Road, Stechford.

The Bull's Head public house, Station Road, *c.* 1900.

The former Bull's Head renamed The Manor public house, 1980. The pub is boarded up at present, and looking in a sorry state.

The Bull's Head, Station Road, *c*. 1903. By the outbreak of the First World War, Stechford was expanding, with buildings appearing in both the upper village of Stechford by the church, and in the lower village towards the Bull's Head.

Flaxley Lane, *c.* 1910. A William Flaxeleye appears on a 1327 subsidy roll, and it is possible that he could be linked to a group of fields, 'The Flaxleys' on the 1847 enclosure map. The 'Leye' of Flaxley tends to confirm that the settlement originated as a clearing in the woods.

Skating on a pool in Flaxley Road.

Flaxley Road during the 1920s. Rose cottage can just be seen at the right-hand side of the row of cottages, just beyond the lamp post.

Rose Cottage, Flaxley Road. As the date above the door shows, the cottage was built in 1876. In 1900, one Joseph Morris, a market gardener, lived at Rose Cottage and it may well be him in this photograph. Rose Cottage was situated in Flaxley Road near to the junction with Station Road.

Flaxley Road and the corner of Station Road in December 1932. Rose Cottage is the first cottage just behind the fencing.

Flaxley Road, December 1932.

Flaxley Road and the corner of Iron Lane, in August 1961.

Constructing McVitie and Price, Flaxley Road, in February 1961.

Atlas Cinema, November 1961. Sir John Smedley Crooke opened the Atlas on Sunday 6 March 1938. In his opening speech he praised the proprietors for providing somewhere for the local people to go. Designed by Ernest Roberts and built by Dare's, a local builder, the opening film was *Cavalcade* staring Dianne Wynyard and Clive Roberts.

Films were shown for over twenty years until closure in 1959, when the cinema was used for wrestling events. These events were not a success and later the building was used as a bingo hall and then a petrol station.

When the cinema first opened in 1938, there was a lot of comment that it was to open on a Sunday and although it had happened for some years elsewhere, Sunday opening was still not widely accepted. I just remember seeing Cliff Richard, in a red jacket, appearing live, before he became famous when I was young. I have to admit I am still a fan.

Flaxley Road, January 1953.

Flaxley Road. The rear entrance to Parkinson Cowan, July 1954.

Flaxley Road, December 1961.

Flaxley Road, 1980. At the turn of the nineteenth century there were still many farms in the area. Fir Tree Farm stood on Flaxley Road, and near the junction of Flaxley Road and Old Farm Road stood Hill House Farm.

Flaxley Road near Stud Lane in December 1932. After the First World War the fields of Stechford began to rapidly disappear under new housing developments.

Church Lane and the corner of Flaxley Road in 1932. Church End Farm could be found near to Church Lane and Flaxley Lane. Church Road Farm stood close to Church Road and Yardley Fields Road.

Stechford River Bridge, *c.* 1910. A significant development in the area was the building of bridges over the River Cole. Since the thirteenth century, bridges over the river at most of the key crossings made it easier for the locals to move about the manor, or to travel to the nearby market towns of Solihull, Coleshill and Birmingham.

Stechford Bridge and the River Cole, 1889. Stycheford Bridge is not referred to until 1497, but a bridge on that site probably dates from much earlier.

45

Stechford Bridge, 1893. Most of the early bridges would have been timber footbridges. Stechford mill and pool lay on the west of the Cole above Stechford Bridge. It was held by Giles de Erdington from 1249-1250 and in the fifteenth century was occupied by the heirs of William West. The mill is shown on eighteenth-century maps and in 1759 John Mockley was the tenant. In 1833, Thomas Smith was tenant but shortly after there is no record of the mill.

Corida service station, Station Road, August 1972.

Station Road in October 1955. The author spent many hours standing at the bus stop in this photograph waiting for the number 11 bus to get to a secondary school in Stockland Green.

Station Road, November 1960. Opposite the number 11 bus stop.

Station Road, between Flaxley Road and Iron Lane. A similar view to the previous, but a more modern view.

Station Road. The entrance to Parkinson Cowan can just be seen on the right-hand side of the photograph. March 1955.

This photograph was taken during the dinner and entertainment in the new Iron Lane building on 30 September 1952. The speaker is Mr H.P. Barker, Managing Director of the Parkinson Cowan Group.

Parkinson Cowan's history started in 1816 when a factory was established in London for the manufacture of 'Wet' gas meters. One of the two pioneers, Samuel Crosby, met up with William Parkinson who was engaged in the coaching business. Parkinson moved to London to work with Crosby. On Crosby's death in 1847, the firm became known as W. Parkinson & Co.

Benjamin Cowan started a business in Glasgow known as 'Gas Meter and Appliance Manufacturers.' The company opened a branch in London in 1873. In 1887, Messrs W. Parkinson & Co. took a licence for manufacturing the first prepayment gas meter. In 1900 the two eldest meter makers came together under the title of Parkinson & W. & B. Cowan. The company opened a Birmingham branch in 1889, and they moved to Stechford in 1912. This was very unpopular with many of the local residents who feared the air would be polluted by the factory.

After the First World War the company was to expand to cover eighteen acres and included a continuous enamelling plant, a large press department and many other facilities. In 1935 a Parkinson cooker was presented to their Majesties King George V and Queen Mary on the occasion of their Silver Jubilee.

Works outing, *c.* 1950. During the Second World War the company modified itself for the products of war. The premises were twice damaged by enemy action and in the second attack two employees were killed. In 1958 the famous 'Prince' range of cookers were developed and produced and – until it was phased out in 1972 – proved to be one of the most popular gas cookers in the country. During its lifetime of fourteen years, over 1,500,000 were built.

Parkinson Cowan Football Club, 1929. In 1971 the company was taken over by Thorn Electric, thereby joining forces with R.A. Main of Edmorton. This made P.C.A. an integral part of the largest group of gas appliance manufacturers in the country. Today the site is a retail park.

British Railways Properties. Cartwright and Company, timber merchants on Station Road and Northcote Road, November 1961.

Station Road looking to Stechford station booking office and the railway bridge. Note the coal lorry turning into Victoria Road. February 1959.

Stechford station and goods yard. Stechford Road railway station opened on the London and Birmingham Line. With the opening of the station the area prospered. Many manufacturers from Aston, Hockley and the jewellery quarter moved to the area as they could now travel to work by train. I remember many a summers evening, when I was young, lying in bed listening to the trains shunting the carriages in the goods yard.

Station Road (undated).

Station Road, January 1960.

54

The corner of Station Road and Manor Road in February 1968.

Manor Road, 1957. The Co-Op bakery can just be seen in the centre of the photograph.

Station Road, 1957.

Station Road, 1957.

Station Road before shops and flats were built, December 1954.

Station Road after the flats and shops had been built, February 1959.

Stechford Road swimming baths.

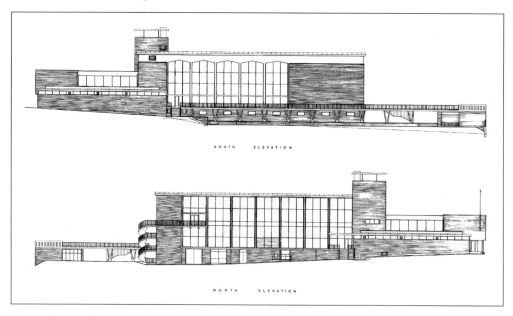

SOUTH ELEVATION

NORTH ELEVATION

An architect's drawing of the proposed swimming baths at Stechford. The architects were A.G. Sheppard Fidler of Birmingham.

The main pool at Stechford swimming baths. The shallow end can be seen and just behind the glass partition was the children's pool. Above the pool is the café.

The lido at Stechford Road baths. The author can remember spending many a Saturday morning splashing about in the water trying to swim. What an excitement when the lido opened and I could spend those warm sunny summer days in the water!

Francis Road, *c.* 1907.

Lyttleton Road. Years ago, if one stood at the top of Lyttleton Road, there were uninterrupted views over fields to Yardley Parish Church. In the other direction fields and country lanes led to Castle Bromwich, Alum Rock and to Bordesley Green.

Corpus Christi Roman Catholic Church, Lyttleton Road. The mission was established in 1919 and mass was said in the presbytery until a temporary church was opened.

The interior of Corpus Christi. The permanent church opened in 1929, and is a rough-cast building consisting of a chancel and an aisled, clerestoried nave.

Stuarts Road.

The corner of Richmond and
Yardley Roads.

Richmond Road.

Skating on a pool in fields behind Field House Farm. A succession of hard winters during the last ten years of the 1800s guaranteed popular winter sports.

Yardley Field Road. Opening of the recreation ground by Councillor W.H. Bulpitt.

Corner of Station Road and Yardley Fields Road, May 1965.

Yardley Fields Road. Most of the farms disappeared after 1945, including Field House Farm, Hill House Farm and Church Road Farm.

Vicarage Road.

Station Road from the corner of Vicarage Road in June 1924.

Three
Glebe Farm

Audley Road, Glebe Farm, October 1965.

Saint Andrew's Church, Audley Road. Saint Andrew's mission was licensed for public worship from 1938.

Audley Road Schools, Audley Road. Today the junior school caters for 352 pupils.

Glebe Farm, (undated). Glebe Farm was originally known as Walters Farm, taking its name from the Walters family. Like many farms in the area it was built in a clearing in the Forest of Arden. The Walters had built a moat around the house.

Glebe Farm, 1932. The farm was situated near to the junction of Church Lane and Kitt's Green Road.

Glebe Farm's outbuildings, November 1932. The farm was to change its name when it was sold to Matthew Boulton. It was then sold to Yardley Parish Church thus becoming a glebe. This is a piece of land serving as part of a clergyman's benefice and providing him with an income.

Glebe Farm. Hay making in the late 1920s. Glebe Farm came into Birmingham in 1911. By the 1920s it was in the tenancy of the Clifts. By the 1930s the farm itself was developed as a council estate with some 1,360 houses. The Riddings, Glebe Farm Road and the Lea Hall estates were built from 1933 onwards.

Hay making on Glebe Farm in the 1920s. New roads such as Audley Road, Kitts Green Road, Wyndhurst Road and Bushbury Road appeared and older roads such as Manor Road, Inglefield Road, Lea Hall Road and Flaxley, Folliott and Mirfields Roads were extended.

Church Road looking down to the Glebe Farm, 1932.

From Church Lane near to the approach to Glebe Farm, December 1932.

Audley Road looking to Glebe Farm Road, December 1963.

Glebe Farm Road, June 1962.

Glebe Farm Road, July 1962.

Glebe Farm Road, August 1969.

74

Glebe Farm Road, August 1969.

The Cock 'n' Bull, Glebe Farm Road.

Glebe Farm Library in June 1952. Glebe Farm Library was opened on 22 April 1952. Constructed of prefabricated reinforced concrete with large windows and glass doors, the new library took a year to build.

Glebe Farm Library. The junior library in June 1952. The building was designed so that extensions could be added easily. The builders were Madocks and Walford Limited.

The adult lending library at Glebe Farm, June 1952. 13,000 books including 2,500 in the children's library, with 6,000 held in reserve, were available at the library, which cost £7,750 to build. Glebe Farm Library was my very first introduction to libraries as a young child, and it was my experiences at this library that convinced me at an early age that I wanted to become a librarian.

Saint Chad's Church.

Glebe Farm Recreational Ground from the bridge near Cole Hall Lane.

Four
Hodge Hill

Hodge Hill Common.

Coleshill Road near Washwood Heath in May 1966.

Coleshill Road looking to Hodge Hill Common, October 1956.

A view along Coleshill Road, May 1966.

Houses on Coleshill Road, November 1972.

Number 25 Coleshill Road, January 1950.

A horse and cart turning into Stechford Road.

Stechford Road looking to Stechford Lane, October 1933.

Stechford Road looking towards Stechford Lane. Compare this with the photograph below when the flats have been built, November 1933.

Stechford Road looking towards Stechford Lane. The same view as above but of a much later date and showing the now-built flats, January 1981.

Stechford Road School. The school opened in 1936 in temporary building accommodation. It opened with permanent accommodation as a junior and infant school in 1937 providing for 288 pupils. In 1954 the school changed its name to Hodge Hill Junior and Infants school and had a total of fourteen classrooms and a hall. The author attended this school and has many fond memories of the buildings and of Mr Barley, the then headmaster. Today the school is known as Colebourne school and caters for 420 pupils. This photograph shows the gatehouse entrance.

The Raven Public House, Hodge Hill Road in February 1956.

Stechford Road at Hodge Hill Common, November 1933. A rental of 1569 names the area known as Hodge Hill as Hidehyll. In his book *One Thousand Years of Birmingham* Carl Chinn suggests that the area could have been named after someone called Hodge. Hodge was a nickname for men called Roger and it later came to be used as the general term for English agricultural labourers.

Hodge Hill Common looking towards Washwood Heath, June 1892. Hodge Hill Common can still be seen today and it became part of Birmingham in 1931. Previously it had belonged to Castle Bromwich.

Hodge Hill Common looking south-east, June 1892.

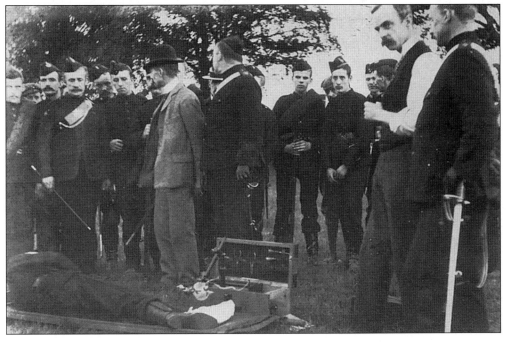

Hodge Hill Common. One of the early x-ray demonstrations given by Dr Hall Edwards who was from the Birmingham General Hospital. The German physicist only discovered this process in 1895, and Rontgen and Hall Edwards were the first to use it for medical x-rays.

Hodge Hill Common looking up Coleshill Road in 1923. The area was developed in the 1920s with mainly private houses being built, on land between Fairholme Road and Colingbourne Road to the west of The Common, between Beaufort Avenue and Buckland's Road to the south, and between Ermington Crescent and Berendale Road to the east.

Hodge Hill Common looking towards Castle Bromwich, 1923. In the 1930s a large housing estate grew up next to the common extending over Buckland End to the south-west. For further information on Shard End, see the book *Castle Vale, Castle Bromwich and Shard End* by M. Baxter and P. Drake in this series.

Hodge Hill Common, 1934. Hodge Hill Farm was situated on the bend of Maggoty Lane, now known as Buckland End Road. The farm was demolished around the 1950s and its land today forms part of the green way along the River Cole.

Hodge Hill Common, September 1959.

Hodge Hill Secondary School. Dining room and gymnasium.

Hodge Hill Secondary School. Entrance Hall.

Five
Washwood Heath

Burney Lane, c. 1911.

BURNEY LANE STECHFORD

Burney Lane, c. 1911. Burney Lane used to be a tiny narrow lane. Two carts could not pass and at the top there were two gates, so when one cart came up it would pull into the gateway so that the other could pass.

Christ Church, Burney Lane, June 1970. Christ Church was consecrated as a Chapel of Ease to Saint Margaret's in 1935. It was designed by H.W. Hobbis and is a brown brick building with stone dressings, a steeply-pitched roof, small round-headed windows and a broad western tower.

CHRIST CHURCH BURNEY LANE WARD END.

Cotterills Lane. Washwood Heath was part of the manor of Saltley and lies on the high ground above the valley of the River Rea. To the east of the boundary was the Wash Brook.

Dancy's Farm, Cottrells Lane, 1923. There are many variations of the meaning of 'waes'; these include a stream for washing sheep or clothes, and land covered with water.

Cottrells Lane, Washwood Heath, May 1925. The earliest reference to the area was in 1454 when it was called 'Wassheworde'. Carl Chinn suggests that this probably indicated the presence of a wood above a wash. Tomlinson's map of Saltley, 1760, shows that for the most part Washwood Heath was uncultivated wasteland or heath.

Fox and Goose public house and Washwood Heath Road, June 1960.

Fox and Goose public house. The Fox and Goose was called the Golden Cross from 1680 to 1780.

Bromford Lane and Washwood Heath Road at the Fox and Goose in March 1932. This road intersection was the terminus of the Number 10 tram from the city and the place where it met the Number 11 Outer Circle bus route.

Coleshill Road and the junctions of Bromford Lane and Washwood Heath Road, May 1966.

The Beaufort Cinema was built at the junction of Bromford Lane and Coleshill Road. The Beaufort was designed by Archibold Hurley Robinson. It opened on 4 August 1929 and was described as Birmingham's Tudor Hall. The architecture was convincing and it was only during demolition that it was discovered that the oak beams were made of plaster. The organ in the cinema was a two manual, eight unit Compton, opened by J.I. Taylor. It was removed to EMI Studios at Saint Johns Wood. In 1937 the auditorium was lengthened at the stage and screen end of the building. The new cinema held seating for 1,548.

The façade of the cinema had three arches, three large windows and a parapet. Alongside the walls inside were mock torch lights and the foyer was covered with lush carpet. The author well remembers watching many a Disney film here in her childhood days. The cinema closed its doors on 10 August 1978 with the film *Warlords From Atlantis*. Demolition soon followed and a DIY store replaced the Beaufort. Today, buildings on the site include a bingo hall and Aldi's food store.

Bromford Lane, May 1966. Washwood Heath became part of Birmingham in 1891.

Bromford Lane and the corner of Fairholme Road in November 1952. In 1802 an event took place in Washwood Heath, which was described as 'the hideous spectacle', by John Alfred Langford. Eight men were publicly executed in April of that year. Six of them were hanged for forgery against the Bank of England and two for burglary at Meriden. It was estimated that some 10,000 people, some travelling many miles, turned out to witness the 'awful scene.'

Bromford Lane near the corner of Saint Margaret's Road, December 1954.

Bromford Lane near the corner of Saint Margaret's Road. The Ideal Service Station, May 1976.

British Road Services buildings at Bromford Lane, January 1960. BRS (or British Road Services) was one of the largest carriers of goods by road in Britain. The Birmingham general haulage offices were in Bromford Lane.

Bromford Lane – the bridge over the River Cole. Looking towards Washwood Heath, June 1952.

Bromford Lane looking towards the railway bridge, June 1952.

Bromford Lane railway bridge, March 1958. The railway station can just be seen next to the billboards and the chimney stack to the centre left of the photograph. The station on the Derby to Birmingham junction railway opened in 1896 for the racecourse traffic.

Bromford Lane, October 1965. Stewarts and Lloyds.

Aston Chain and Hook, Bromford Lane, March 1956.

The rail bridge over the River Tame with Stewarts and Lloyds in the background. April 1955.

Stewarts and Lloyds on Bromford Lane. Wheelwright Road can just be seen turning to the left. April 1955.

Stewarts and Lloyds, Bromford Lane, April 1955. Stewarts and Lloyds was one of the largest tube manufacturing concerns in the world. The Bromford Lane section made seamless tubes and lighting columns.

Entrance to Stewarts and Lloyds on Bromford Lane. April 1955.

Bromford Lane and Wheelwright Road, pictured in September 1954.

Drews Lane looking towards Washwood Heath Road. Another narrow lane, like Burney lane but a little wider because of the carts going to the mill. Drews Lane had its own water mill from around 1425 and, in fact, the road was known in its early days as Mill Lane. In 1858 John Drew from Edgbaston developed a water-powered flour mill there. Later the firm moved to Perry Barr, but John Drew gave his name to the road. The mill was remembered as a picturesque mill with the pool being in a field at the back. The mill was part of the Ward End Estate. The mill was pulled down soon after the First World War. The millpond was to become allotments and the site disappeared when the first council houses were built in the 1920s.

Ward End timber supply, F. James and Sons, Drews Lane. The building was known as Cocksparrow Hall. In the early fifteenth century it was a gamekeepers cottage, and in more modern times an old lady lived there who sold sweets to the local children.

The corner of Drews Lane and Washwood Heath Road looking towards Castle Bromwich, October 1926.

Wolseley Works, Drews Lane. Home-time for the workforce. The Wolseley Tool and Motor Company Limited, under the auspices of Vickers Sons and Maxim was set up at Adderley Park in 1901. In the first year Wolseley built 323 cars at the Birmingham factory.

Wolseley Works. One shift arrives as another leaves. The Birmingham factory had been constructed in 1897 for Stanley Brothers and Westwood Limited who were in the cycle trade.

Building the Wolseley cars. By 1909 Wolseley were building engines for railcars, aircraft and marine use. After the Second World War, a second plant was taken over; the Drews Lane site in Ward End. This factory had originally been built by a Vickers subsidiary in 1913.

Wolseley Works. In 1940, the Ward End factories made shells, Bren carriers, mines and Horsa gliders, despite serious bomb damage sustained in 1941.

The shop floor at Wolseley Works.

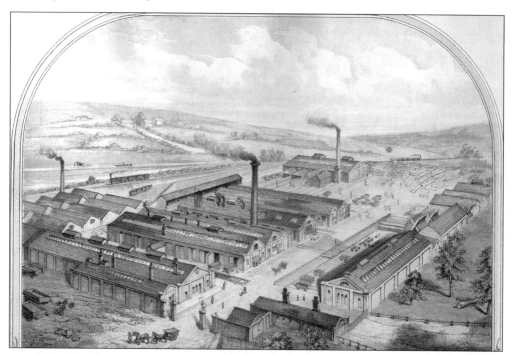

J. Wright & Sons, Railway Carriage and Wagon works, Drews Lane. The origins of Metro-Cammell go back to the stage coaches, which used to provide passenger and stage coach services. Joseph Wright foresaw that the railways, which were appearing in 1830, would replace the stage coach so he diverted from the manufacturing of the coaches to the manufacturing of rail carriages. In 1845, six acres of meadow was acquired and the factory was built. The company of Metropolitan Railway Carriage and Wagon Company Limited was formed in 1862. So began over one hundred and fifty years of rolling stock manufacturing in the area.

Six
Ward End

Five Fields, Ward End.

The Barley Mow. The Domesday Book of 1086 shows that the area we know as Ward End was part of Little Bromwich in the parish of Aston. There have been various spellings of Ward End; in around 1460 it was 'Warde End' and in 1658 'Wardende'. The name Ward End was first recorded in 1460.

Ward End Hall, c. 1900. Ward End has had its fair share of large houses including Ward End Hall and Ward End House.

Ward End Hall. This stood back from Black Pitts Lane, the road now called Saint Margaret's Avenue. The house was reputedly built in 1710. Various members of the Hutton family (related to William Hutton, the famous Birmingham historian) lived at Ward End Hall for a number of years. The house was demolished after the Second World War to make way for flats.

Ward End Hall site. Proposed multi-storey flats, designed by Herbert Manzoni.

House in Ward End Park, 1934. Ward End House, or the Park House, also known as the White House, was the home of the Marshall family, who were bankers. George William Marshall the genealogist was born at the house in 1839. He sold the house to Frederick Gwyther in 1884. On his death in 1891, his widow continued to live in the house until 1895. A year later she remarried and the house and part of the land was sold to Birmingham Corporation in 1903.

The official opening of Ward End Park in May 1904. The eastern side of the city was in great need of recreational space and in 1903 Birmingham City Council purchased forty-two acres for £313,514. With Ward End House and its eleven acres purchased from C.E. Jachinchen for £7,500 Ward End Park opened in 1904.

Ward End Park. Awaiting the arrival of the Right Honourable Joseph Chamberlain on the occasion of his seventieth birthday celebrations in July 1906.

The seventieth birthday celebrations of the right Honourable Joseph Chamberlain. Mr and Mrs Chamberlain at Ward End Park, July 1906.

Children outside the entrance to Ward End Park, *c.* 1907.

The bandstand in Ward End Park.

Ward End Park. A large ornamental boating pool fed by natural springs was constructed in the winter of 1908/09. A plaque commemorates the event with the following 'The Construction of this Boating Pool was Undertaken By The City Council To Provide Relief Work For Unemployed Men Of The City during The Winter 1908-1909.'

Ward End Park. The boating pool starts to take shape.

Ward End Park boating pool. An aviary and winter garden were added to the park in 1914.

Ward End Park boating pool. Gary, a local lad, remembers throwing sticks into the brook which runs through Ward End Park and following them until they came to a grating at the park boundary. He then discovered that he could get through the grating. The dark tunnel led to a path on Common Lane by the Metro-Cammell works. The tunnel became known to the local lads as 'the dark half hour' because of the time it took to crawl along it.

Ward End Park. The floral clock was a feature in the park for many years. In this photograph, the Centenary of the City of Birmingham Parks Department is depicted. In the background, the building on the left is Maitland Hall, the Conservative Club.

Leigh Road School. The school was opened in 1909 with 1,000 pupils. Altered and reorganised in 1931, the senior boys school became a separate school to the junior and infants' school. The practical block of the senior school was destroyed by enemy action during the Second World War. The school changed its name in 1954 to Leigh Boys' County Modern School.

The official opening of Ward End Library.

Ward End Library, 1931.

Treaford Hall. William Ward sold the estates of Treaford Hall in 1850. The manor house stood on the north side of Alum Rock Road and west of its junction with Sladefield Road. By 1848 it was owned by W. Webb Essington and occupied by Isaac Marshall. In 1911 the house, known as the Moat House, became a convent of the Anglical Society of the Incarnation on the Eternal Son, which ran boys' orphanages.

Houses near the church, Ward End, 1934.

Ward End Church, 1934.

Ward End Chapel. Thomas Boyd, a merchant from Coventry, built the first church shortly after 1517. By 1730 the chapel was in ruins.

An ironmonger from Birmingham, Mr Blackman, repaired the chapel but by the early nineteenth century it was in ruins again. A successful appeal for rebuilding was launched in 1833, and the new church was dedicated in 1834.

Saint Margaret's Church, 1891. Pevsner describes the church as 'a small and simple building of chancel, nave and west tower in the thin Gothic of its period, of brick with stone dressing, but painted inside and rendered to simulate ashlar.' The new church was consecrated in 1941.

Saint Mark's Church. The church was licensed for worship as a Chapel of Ease of Saint Saviour's in1890. The building is of red brick with stone dressings and was consecrated in 1899. The architect was J.A. Chatwin.

Saint Mark's Church house. The architect was H. Hobbis.

Penley Grove.

Ingleton Road Schools. The council school was opened in 1931 by Birmingham City Council. It accommodated 532 pupils. Damaged by enemy action in 1941, the school was repaired by 1953. The name was changed in 1954 to Ward End Primary School.

Sladefield Road, March 1931.

Washwood Heath Road. In 1250 Washwood Heath Road was a winding road from Birmingham to Coleshill but by 1759 it was a turnpike road with toll gates.

Washwood Heath Road.

Arley Road and the corner with
Washwood Heath Road.